CARD
GAMES

CARD
GAMES

A BULFINCH PRESS BOOK
Little, Brown and Company
Boston · Toronto · London

First United States Edition

ISBN 0-8212-1973-1

Library of Congress Catalog Card Number 92-52969

Library of Congress Cataloging-in-Publication
information is available.

Bulfinch Press is an imprint and trademark of
Little, Brown and Company (Inc.)

Editorial Director: MADAME JOANNA LORENZ
Creative Director: SIR PETER BRIDGEWATER
Text: PAUL BARNETT & RON TINER ESQUIRES
Original Illustrations: COLONEL IVAN HISSEY

The Publishers particularly wish to thank Cartes France
for supplying some of the illustrations for this book.

The Publishers would like to thank all those who kindly
gave permission to use visual materials in this book.

PRINTED IN HONG KONG

CONTENTS

AN IMPORTANT WORD of
WARNING 6

SOLITAIRES and PATIENCE GAMES

TOAD in the HOLE 12

DISLOYAL TRAVELLERS 14

PUSS in the CORNER 16

DEMON 20

BELEAGUERED CASTLE 24

THE WINDMILL 29

COMPETITIVE GAMES

PELMANISM 36

PIQUET 40

WHIST 48

SOLO WHIST 58

BEZIQUE 64

OLD SLEDGE 68

CALIFORNIA LOO 72

KLABBERJASS 74

BLACK LADY HEARTS 78

CANASTA 82

FAN TAN 88

GLOSSARY:
The Language of Card Players 92

AN IMPORTANT WORD of **WARNING** from the AUTHOR

Many people regard cards with suspicion – Dean Swift described them as the **"Devil's Books"** – and they are right to do so; for cards have led countless unfortunates down the slippery slope into degradation and depravity; the vileness of Mr. Acton Bell's notorious TENANT* may have been born from strong liquor, but cards, too, played their role in his sorry downfall. ☞

But such *Evils* cannot be ascribed to cards in themselves; the Sinners are not the cards or even the games but the men – yes, and it must be said: sometimes women – who are the players! They who choose to wager on the fall of the cards must know that they are gambling with that *Enemy* who is the *Foe to All Men;* and that a *Dreadful Price* will be exacted. ☜

The games I have chosen for you here are wholesome, and **may be indulged in by all**, even the young, except, that is, on the *Lord's Day*, when we must all have Other, and Higher, Duties. But on the secular days of our week, let us recall the words of Dr. Saml. Johnson, that . . . *to play at cards . . . is very useful in life: it generates kindness and consolidates society.*

ARMYTAGE WARE M.A. (OXON), D.D.
(ST. ANDREWS), BOXING DAY, 1899

* The Author refers to a leading character in the romantic novel *The Tenant of Wildfell Hall*, and may have been unaware that Acton Bell was the *nom de plume* of Anne Brontë (1820–1849).

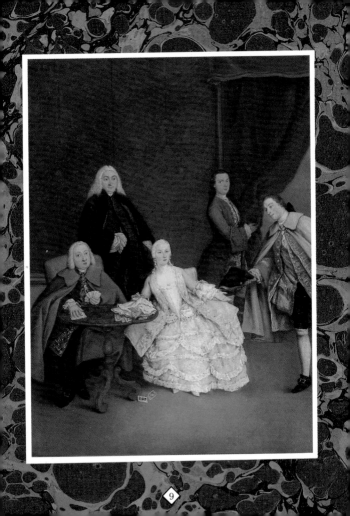

SOLITAIRES and
PATIENCE GAMES
to Quicken the Mind
and CHALLENGE THE
CONCENTRATION

TOAD IN THE HOLE
~

FOR THIS EXCELLENT game we require two full packs, well shuffled together. Our aim is to assemble eight piles of cards, in sequential order from Ace (or One) to King; regardless of their suit. To begin, we must deal 13 cards as our RESERVE; they are placed in a pile, face upwards, the topmost card only being available for our use after play commences. If any of these 13 cards are Aces, they should be placed in a row to the right of the reserve pile as our initial FOUNDATION cards; failing that, we must find an Ace among the remaining cards, which are our STOCK. Whenever an Ace shall appear in play, it must be used to become a foundation card.

In play, we turn up one card at a time from our stock. Should it be possible to play the card on to a foundation pile; then that we must do. Otherwise, the card should be placed on one of the WASTE PILES,  of which there are five; we may place the cards in any order in the waste piles; we shall engage one waste pile for **COURT CARDS**, so that lower-order cards are not early lost to us. Should a waste pile be exhausted, the next card turned up from stock must be placed there (so that there are always five in play); but the reserve pile is not to be thus replenished.

The game is over once all 104 cards are used, and no further play is possible; or, the game is "lost" if all the *stock* is used and no cards at the top of the *waste* piles or *reserve* can be played.

DISLOYAL TRAVELLERS

~

Kings are our foes in this game; but perhaps that petty treason is permissible to us in the Age of a glorious Queen. We deal out the shuffled cards of a pack, face downwards, to form twelve piles, each of four cards, in three rows; the first pile is allocated for the Aces, the second for the Deuces, and so until the twelfth, for the Queens; we must arrange our cards so that each heap be in its fitting place. The remaining four cards are our **TRAVELLERS.**

We turn up our first TRAVELLER. Say it should be a Knave, or JACK. We place the Knave face-up at the bottom of the eleventh heap, then turn up the top card of that heap. Say this is a SEVEN; we place it under the seventh pile, whose top card we now turn up. We continue thus until we should turn up a King; which card we must cast aside, drawing a new card from our TRAVELLERS to restart our game. Our aim is to finish with all four cards in all twelve piles face up before us, but should our Kings be ill disposed then failure will be our lot.

PUSS *in the* CORNER

We need to be as sly as a cat to succeed in this game! For in its playing, ART is as staunch an ally as FORTUNE!

We start by placing the four Aces as *foundations* in a square; the remaining cards are our *stock*, and we must use these to build upon the foundations sequentially from Ace (or One) to King; although we need follow the colours of the cards only, so that Diamonds go with Hearts, and Clubs with Spades. We turn up one card from stock at a time; a card that cannot be used to build upon a foundation is placed upon one of four *waste packets* or *piles* at the square's corners; the topmost card of a waste pile may later be used at will. Once all cards be in play, the waste heaps, unshuffled, are gathered into a single pack in the order of our choice which is turned face down and used again as stock (tho' only once); but now we may use only one waste packet. The game is won if all the cards can be used up to form the requisite sequences. The ART is in the wise placing of cards into the waste piles!

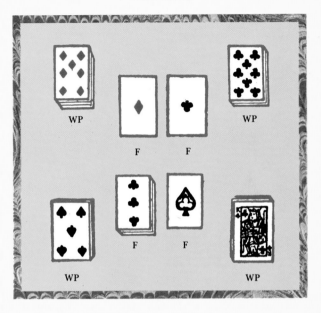

F: Foundation   WP: Waste pile

*During the first part of Play
(only one waste pile is allowable
in the latter stages)*

17

DEMON

SEVERAL GAMES OF PATIENCE are described as *"Demon,"* but this is one much used in Scotland; where doubtless success in the enterprise is greeted with copious libations; but we need not emulate the Caledonians!

We aim to create four packets, or PILES, in each the sequence running from Ace (or One) to King of the same suit. We take a single pack, very well shuffled. We must first deal out *thirteen* cards as our RESERVE, and place these face downwards to one side. Then, from the STOCK in our hand, in which the remaining cards are held face downwards, we lay out, side-by-side, and face upwards, five cards that are to be the first cards of our COLUMNS. Should any of these be an Ace, we place it instead in one of the four SEQUENCE PILES, one for each suit, that we shall build above the columns; and draw a new ☞

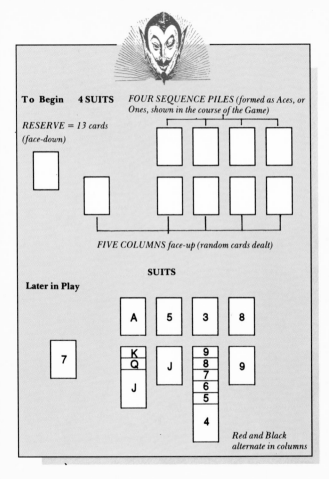

To Begin 4 SUITS   *FOUR SEQUENCE PILES (formed as Aces, or Ones, shown in the course of the Game)*

RESERVE = 13 cards
(face-down)

FIVE COLUMNS face-up (random cards dealt)

SUITS

Later in Play

Red and Black alternate in columns

⟨21⟩

card from the RESERVE to replace it.

The mode of play is thus. Draw *three cards* from the stock and turn them over together

so that only one shows. This card we may use in one of two ways. **FIRST**, it may be added to a sequence pile, should it be the next in ascending order of the relevant suit. **SECOND**, it may be added to one of the columns; these are formed in descending order and in alternating colours; thus below the Queen of Spades might be the Knave or *Jack,* of Diamonds and then the Ten of Clubs; and so on. Should the stock card be used, the next card thus exposed may be used; otherwise, draw *three* more cards, as before. Individual cards may be moved from columns to sequence piles or

whole columns joined together (by the act, for example, of moving a column headed by a red Seven to descend from a column ended by a black Eight) and whenever a column becomes vacant a fresh card is drawn from the *reserve* to re-start that column; otherwise no cards may be withdrawn from the reserve (the game is lost, of course, should it prove impossible to utilize all of the reserve cards). Any Ace, whenever exposed, is used as foundation for its suit's sequence pile. When the stock is exhausted, it is turned over and re-used *ad infinitum*.

Two people may use two packs to play this game in competition as *"Racing Demon."* Each may add to or take from the other's columns. Fast wits are required; and beware! for *Tempers may Fray!*

BELEAGUERED CASTLE

As with many Solitaires, our intention is to create four **SEQUENCE PILES**, one per each suit, ascending from Ace (or One) to King. First we extract from our pack, and lay out, one above the other and face upwards, the four Aces for use as **FOUNDATIONS**. Next we shuffle the rest of the pack and set out the *"wings"* of our game to left and right of each Ace; each "wing" is of six cards, dealt face upwards, the cards partially obscuring each other such that only the outermost in each "wing" is fully exposed and thus available for play. Exposed cards may be moved on to one of the growing sequence piles, singly or in sequence, or to the end of a different "wing," the "wings" being increased by a downward succession, regardless of suit; so that a Queen must follow a King and so on. Should a "wing" be all used up, any exposed card may be moved to the space to start a new "wing."

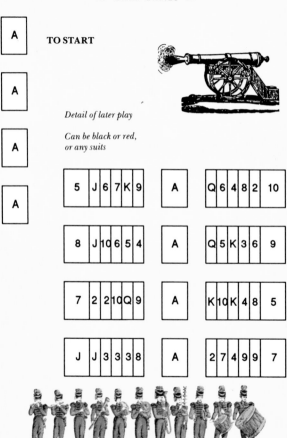

TO START

Detail of later play

*Can be black or red,
or any suits*

A
A
A
A

5	J	6	7	K	9

A

Q	6	4	8	2	10

8	J	10	6	5	4

A

Q	5	K	3	6	9

7	2	2	10	Q	9

A

K	10	K	4	8	5

J	J	3	3	3	8

A

2	7	4	9	9	7

THE WINDMILL

One glance at the way the cards are arrayed for this game betrays why it is named **THE WINDMILL**! We shall require two packs, well shuffled, but separate one from the other; our aim is to create one packet or pile of fifty-two cards, running *up* from Ace (or One) to King four times, and four packets or piles, running *down* from King to Ace in each instance; no regard is to be paid to suit in either instance. Initially we use but the one pack. First we place an Ace centrally, and then we set two cards to each edge of this first card, to form a cross; the remaining cards of the pack are our *STOCK*. The cards at the end of the "*sails*" are available for play. Should a Deuce be at the end of a "sail," it may be placed on the central Ace, followed by a Trey, and so on. A King will be set in one of the interstices betwixt the sails.

We deal out the first pack, one by one, face upwards, on to a WASTE PILE, drawing upon the cards where it is possible to add to any of the sequences being formed; ☞

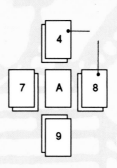

START

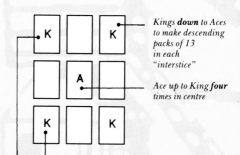

*Kings **down** to Aces to make descending packs of 13 in each "interstice"*

*Ace up to King **four** times in centre*

POSITION OF KINGS (as they appear)

LATER IN PLAY

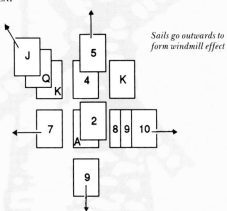

Sails go outwards to form windmill effect

also replenishing the "sails" when need be. From the first pack we must not add to the central pile beyond the first Queen. We may add to the downward sequences at will, though we are not obliged to; it can be helpful not to be too ready, at an early stage, to add to these piles; the topmost card of one of these side-piles may be moved to the centre, but not *VICE VERSA*.

The second pack is now to be treated as the first, except in that further cards beyond the Queen may now be added to the central pile. Once our stock has been exhausted into the waste pile, the waste pile may be turned and re-used once only. The game is lost if all five piles are *not* formed.

nd Flower

Joueurs.

COMPETITIVE GAMES
for *Pleasure,*
Amusement and WHOLESOME
FAMILY ENTERTAINMENT

PELMANISM

HIS IS A MEMORY GAME for all members of the family – any number may play – and, until the foundation last year of the Pelman Institute for Scientific Development of Mind Memory, it was more commonly called CONCENTRATION; but Progress changes all things.

All the cards are laid out face downwards, in rows or a circle. The first player selects at random two cards, which he turns up, and shows to the other players, before replacing them face downwards, as before. However, should the two cards be of the same numbers value – two Sevens, shall we say, or two Knaves or *Jacks* – he retains them as a TRICK and has another play. The next player selects a single card; if it makes a pair with one of those just replaced, then he, too, may make a trick by turning up one of those (if the player can but *remember* where lies the matching card!), and then draw another card; but if he misremembers, and so turns up a wrong second card, both cards are replaced; and it is the next player's turn; and so on. The winner is he who holds

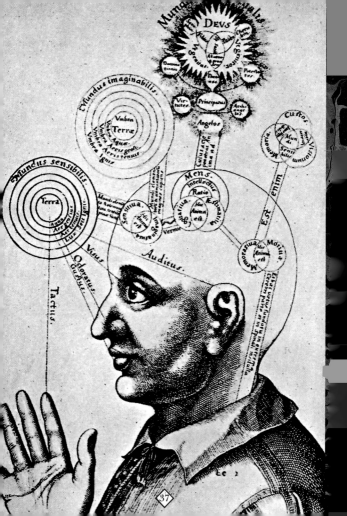

the greatest number of tricks when all the cards are gone.

PELMANISM may be played with any number of packs, and if more than four players wish to participate then at least two packs are recommended to increase the enjoyment (the packs bearing identical designs and colouring on their backs to preserve the confusion in the players' minds). The *American* version of this game (called "Concentration") allows each player to pick up *2* cards at each play.

PIQUET

PIQUET *is a game for two players; victory is determined through scoring points, so paper and pencil are necessary. The pack used is the* PIQUET PACK *of thirty-two cards, the* DEUCES, TREYS, FOURS, FIVES *and* SIXES *having been excised from a standard pack. The game has no trumps. After cutting for the dealership, the Dealer gives himself and his opponent – this latter called the* ELDER HAND *– each a hand of twelve cards, dealt out in twos or threes; the other eight cards are put face downwards between them as the* STOCK. *Now the first stage of the game, known as the* CALLING, *begins.*

Should either player have no Royal Cards at all, he must cry: **"Carte Blanche!"** and he scores ten points. The Elder Hand must now discard at least one and up to five cards from his hand, replenishing from the stock; should he elect to exchange fewer than five cards, he may look at those — without showing the Dealer — that he has declined. His rejected cards take no further part in the play. The Dealer must now do likewise (tho' there may be insufficient stock cards for him to take as many as five). Then the "calling" begins in earnest. There are THREE CATEGORIES in which points may be scored.

The first is called the **POINT**. The Elder Hand declares the most number of cards he has in any one suit; should the Dealer have more in any suit than this, he says: "Not Good," and scores as many points as he has cards in his longest suit; should he have fewer, he says: "Good," and the Elder Hand scores as would have the Dealer. Should the Dealer have the same number, he says: "Equal;" the pips on those cards in both hands are counted (at face value, but with Royal Cards ☙

counting as ten, and Aces or Ones as eleven), and the player with more cards scores one point for each card. At NO STAGE during the "calling" does the Dealer declare to the Elder Hand how many points he (the Dealer) is accumulating, though the points from the Elder Hand are mutually known.

The next category is the **SEQUENCE**. The Elder Hand offers the longest consecutive run of cards he has, above three, in a single suit, scoring three points for a sequence of three cards, four for a sequence of four, but fifteen for a sequence of five, sixteen for a sequence of six, and so on. The Dealer responds with "Not Good," "Good," or "Equal," as before; also as before, pips are counted to establish supremacy should the Dealer have said: "Equal," and, if the pips are of equal value, neither scores. The player with the best single sequence also scores points for all the other sequences in his hand, the points being counted as for "longest sequence."

Third is the declaration of **QUA-TORZES** and **TRIOS**. Here only TENS, KNAVES or JACKS, QUEENS, KINGS, and ACES are tallied. Four of these cards alike (a **quatorze**) scores fourteen points; three (a **trio**) scores three points. Four Aces defeat four Kings, and so on. The player whose cards are "Good" then scores points also, to the same level, for any other **quatorze** or **trio** he may possess, while his opponent scores naught. ❧

Now play commences. The Elder Hand plays a card, and the Dealer must then proclaim his tally of points from the categories listed above. The Dealer must then attempt to win the first TRICK by playing a card of higher value, but of the same suit. The winner of the first trick initiates the second, and so until the cards are done. The player instigating each play scores a point for so doing; should he lose the trick, his opponent gains a point. The taker of the last trick scores an extra point. The player with the more tricks at the end gains an additional ten points "for the cards;" but if both players have six tricks, no points are scored; and if one player takes all the tricks (a **CAPOT**) he adds forty points to his score.

If neither player has a **CARTE BLANCHE**, two other happenstances may lead to the gaining of additional points. If one player scores thirty points during "calling" without the other having scored at all, he gains a further sixty points; this is a **REPIQUE**. And, once play has started, if the Elder Hand's total attains thirty points before the Dealer has scored at all, he adds a further thirty points; this is a **PIQUE**.

Clearly, since the Elder Hand scores for laying the first card, it would be impossible for the Dealer to gain a **PIQUE**.

Participants play six hands in what is called a **PARTIE**, at the end of which the player with the highest total of points is the winner. The rules for scoring have been corrupted by such sorry souls as have adopted this game for gambling; but that is only meet, for those BASE PEOPLE are corrupting themselves, too, by their actions.

WHIST

Who **knows when** *WHIST* was born? It seems that this game must be as old as playing cards themselves; certes, few of the more genteel families in our realm cannot have whiled away a pleasant hour in this most respectable of pastimes. I am proud to say that it was introduced to me by no less illustrious a personage than *Bishop Saml. Wilberforce* himself; cruel the horse that threw him!

Whist is a game for four players, playing in two partnerships, with the partners sitting opposite each other; a single pack of fifty-two cards is used. Our aim is to score points, primarily through the **WINNING** of **TRICKS**. A Dealer, having been initially selected by cutting or otherwise, deals out

the cards in rotation – all but the last, which is placed face upwards in the centre, and the suit of which denotes the suit that will be *TRUMPS* for this hand. Cards in the *trump* suit for each hand assume more power than their more humble brethren, as will be seen. Thus, at the start of the game, the Dealer has but twelve cards, while all the rest have thirteen; but, as soon as the first trick has been played, he will expropriate that exposed card to his own hand.

The player to the Dealer's *left* is the first to lay a card; and play proceeds clockwise. It is incumbent upon the other participants, if they are able to, to lay cards in response to this first that are of the same suit; the player of the highest-value card, should all succeed in following suit, would thereby take the trick. How-ever, commonly, a player is unable to follow suit, and then he must do one of two things, *viz:* he may discard that which is of little value to him or, he deems, to his partner; *or* he may elect to lay a card of the trump suit, which will take the trick unless a later player, also unable to follow the leading suit, determines to present a trump card of higher value. The player that takes the trick leads for the next one; and so on until all the cards are done.

Should a player *inadvertently expose a card*, that card must remain exposed until his opponents command him to play it. This penalty is particularly salutary when *CHILDREN* are participating in the game, for it cures them rapidly of that carelessness to which the youth of this age are so sadly prone.

Partners are not allowed to communicate with each other, either by word or by gesture; thus alertness is of paramount importance in the playing of whist; for only through a close attention to the cards that are played can one partner gain an

impression of the cards that yet remain in his partner's hand; and if partners are incapable of establishing such a *RAPPORT*, as the French call it, then their efforts are likely to be haphazard.

A successful partnership, it must be iterated, is one in which both partners are able to perceive and *INTUIT* the significance of each card that is placed on the table; and thus make full use of the combined strengths of their two hands.

At the end of each game, points are awarded in four manners. The first is through the gaining of **TRICKS**. The first six tricks gained by the winning partnership do not count for points at all; they are known as the "*book*," and each trick taken in excess of the "*book*" gains the partnership a point (so if a total of nine tricks are taken, the partnership gains but three points).

Second, there are **HONOURS** points: these are awarded as recognition that a partnership has held an abundance of Royal Cards in the trump suit; thus if the partnership holds the Ace, King, Queen and Knave or *Jack* of the trump suit, it is granted four honours points; and if it holds three of these cards it gains three points; but no honours points are granted for fewer than three. Third, a **PENALTY** inflicted upon the opponents may gain points for a partnership. Should a player have laid a wrong-suited card

in a trick when he possessed a correctly suited card that he might have played, he is guilty of a *REVOKE*; and the opposing partnership receives three points. And, finally, fourth: at the end of each game additional points may be scored by the *Victorious Partnership* to acknowledge the poor performance of the vanquished. Three additional points are given should the opponents have scored no game points; two, should they 🍂

have attained but a miserly one or two game points; and one should they have achieved only three or four game points.

At the end of each game, the Dealership passes to the next player in a *CLOCKWISE* direction. The cards are, of course, thoroughly shuffled and cut before the commencement of the next game. A set of three games is decreed to be a **RUBBER**; and it is the consistent winning of rubbers, rather than the aimless taking of an occasional game, that demarcates the truly strong partnership.

SOLO
WHIST

Although there are four players in this variation of *Whist,* it is not essentially a partnership game, being generally a question of every man for himself. Play is generally as in Whist, but with bidding varied as below. Although sneered upon by some as being ARRIVISTE, to use a foreign word for lack of a plain one, *Solo Whist,* or *Solo,* is regarded by many – especially among the youthful, the flighty, and the ebullient (it is primarily a ladies' game) – as being yet more enthralling than its parent, boasting as it does a plethora of different options for progress. Myself, I find it *amusing* enough.

Nonce-rules may soon be derived should it prove impracticable to have four players, so that three or five participate;

but for our present purposes I assume that at least some semblance of order and gravity is being maintained. Once the party has settled itself and a *Dealer* has been selected by cutting, he passes the players (including himself, of course) their cards in GROUPS OF THREE, until there are but four cards remaining to him; of which he gives one card to each of his three fellows, then turns up the last card to determine the TRUMP SUIT. He will pick it up for his own hand once the first trick has been taken.

The players study the cards that *FORTUNE* has allotted them; and then the first player CLOCKWISE from the *Dealer* "**calls**;" that is to say: declares his intentions. He has eight choices of call, *VIZ* (in increasing order of priority): – Should he say – "*Pass*," this signifies that he has no specific intentions for this hand. Should all the players say: "Pass," then the hand is abandoned and another dealt. "*I propose*" is a  🖙

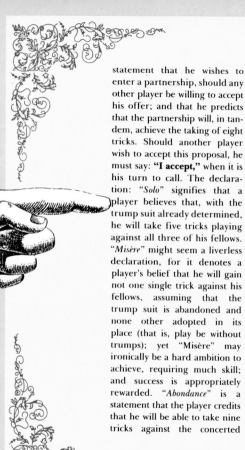

statement that he wishes to enter a partnership, should any other player be willing to accept his offer; and that he predicts that the partnership will, in tandem, achieve the taking of eight tricks. Should another player wish to accept this proposal, he must say: **"I accept,"** when it is his turn to call. The declaration: *"Solo"* signifies that a player believes that, with the trump suit already determined, he will take five tricks playing against all three of his fellows. *"Misère"* might seem a liverless declaration, for it denotes a player's belief that he will gain not one single trick against his fellows, assuming that the trump suit is abandoned and none other adopted in its place (that is, play be without trumps); yet *"Misère"* may ironically be a hard ambition to achieve, requiring much skill; and success is appropriately rewarded. *"Abondance"* is a statement that the player credits that he will be able to take nine tricks against the concerted

efforts of his fellows; as assistance, he will have the right to determine a new trump suit, and need not declare what it is until the first card of the hand is about to be laid. "*Abondance in trumps*" means the same, but using the trump already nominated. "*Misère Ouverte*" signifies that the player will succeed in taking not one single trick, even though, after the first trick has been played, his cards will be laid out for the others to see. Finally, "*Abondance Déclarée,*" the grandest of all declarations, is a statement of intent to take all thirteen tricks; here the player may not only decide the trump suit but also has the right to lay the first card of the hand (in all other cases, the player to the Dealer's left leads).

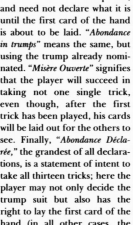

The scoring system is complicated; and some parties use CHEQUERS to assist them; but chequers are but a step away from coins and so I strongly recommend keeping the score using paper and pencil.

For a successful *PARTNER-SHIP*, each partner receives a point, and a point is subtracted from any earlier score each of the other two players might have; this applies also to each additional trick won above the eight declared. An unsuccessful partnership forfeits points on the same scale. A successful *SOLO* gains two points from each adversary, plus a further point for each over-trick. A successful *MISÈRE* gains three points from each opponent; a *MISÈRE OUVERTE* six; with a penalty point deductible for each trick inadvertently taken. The two *ABONDANCES* merit four points; and an *ABONDANCE DÉCLARÉE* is rewarded with eight.

There are no formal rubbers, as in whist. The game merely continues until the company tires of it, and turns instead to more *Improving Pastimes*.

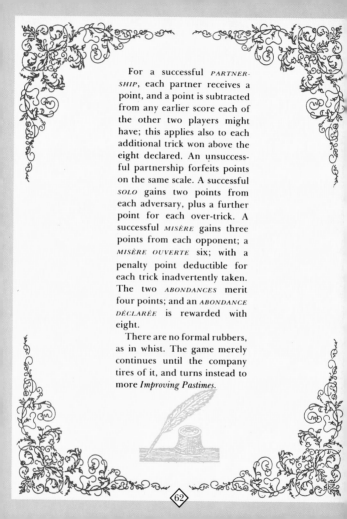

Bézique

AS FOR *PIQUET*, which is likewise a game for two players, in *Bézique* all cards of LESSER value than the Sevens must be discarded prior to commencing; however, unlike *Piquet*, two packs are required for play, the sixty-four remaining cards of the packs being shuffled together. Another difference is in the ranking of the cards, for in descending order this runs: ACE, TEN, KING, QUEEN, KNAVE OR *JACK*, NINE, EIGHT, SEVEN. Finally, in *Bézique* there is a *TRUMP SUIT*; whereas in *Piquet* there is none.

The Dealer is selected by cutting for the higher card (with the Ten ranking above all but the Ace). He deals eight cards to his opponent and to himself (as to three cards, and then two cards, and then three cards), and places the remaining cards, face downwards, between them as the STOCK; but the top card of the stock pile is turned up to determine the **TRUMP SUIT**. Should this card be a Seven, the Dealer is forthwith awarded a gratuitous ten points.

The purpose of *Bézique* is to take TRICKS containing certain scoring cards that are known as *BEZIQUES*, and also to make winning combinations of certain cards. The "*Elder Hand*" – that is to say, the player who is not the Dealer – lays the first card, and the two participants play for tricks rather as one might in whist; except that, with the exemption of the trump suit itself, the suits are ignored: only the relative values of the cards are important. Should cards of equal value be played, the trick is deemed to be taken by the player who led.

Before play continues after the completion of each trick, its winner may make one (AND ONLY ONE) of the declarations listed beneath; as he does so he must lay the respective cards on the table in front of him; he is awarded points as shown:

THE SEVEN OF TRUMPS	*10 points*
A COMMON MARRIAGE	
(the King and Queen of a non-trump suit)	*20 points*
A ROYAL MARRIAGE	
(the King and Queen of the trump suit)	*40 points*
A SINGLE BÉZIQUE	
(the Queen of Spades and Knave of Diamonds)	*40 points*
A DOUBLE BÉZIQUE	
(the Queen of Spades and Knave	
of Diamonds attained for the second	
time by the same player)	*500 points*
FOUR KNAVES OR "JACKS"	*40 points*
FOUR QUEENS	*60 points*
FOUR KINGS	*80 points*
FOUR ACES	*100 points*
FIVE BEST TRUMPS	
(Ace, Ten, King, Queen, Knave)	*250 points*

In addition, a trick containing an Ace or a Ten is called a *BRISQUE*, and gains its winner a further 10 points. The cards laid out face upwards in front of a player may continue to be used by that player for tricks as the game progresses.

Once the declaration is over, each of the players takes a card from the top of the stock; and play continues as above until but one of the stock cards remains, and the trump-card; the winner of the last trick before this takes the stock card, and the loser the trump-card. Eight further tricks are now played before the hand is deemed done; for these the players must follow suit if feasible, and certainly may not trump should they have cards available with which to follow suit; and the winner of the last trick gains ten additional points.

The winner of the game is the player who first attains a predetermined number of points; four thousand points is customary, but a goal of two thousand points is becoming increasingly common as the pace of life increases and we have less time for our *RELAXANT DIVERSIONS*.

OLD SLEDGE

This is a game much enjoyed by children at Christmas, which is perhaps why it gained its undignified, but coyly charming, sobriquet; it is known also as *"SEVEN UP," "HIGH-LOW JACK," "ALL FOURS,"* and other names besides. Yet it is not exclusively a recreation for the **immature**; and adults, too, may use it to while away their time. It may be played by two or by three players; or, with a little variation, by four. The object of the enterprise is to amass seven points through obtaining certain cards and through winning *TRICKS. A full pack of fifty-two cards is employed.*

After a dealership is established, through cutting, the Dealer makes for each player a hand of six cards, three by three. The next card is turned up to determine the *TRUMP SUIT.* (Should the card be a

Knave or "Jack," the Dealer is immediately awarded one point.) The player to the Dealer's left may now challenge the trump suit; should he not wish to do so, he says: "Stand;" but if he would prefer another he should say; "I beg," at which the Dealer may elect to stand by the trump suit already nominated (in which instance he must say: "Take one," and award the player one point), or he may prefer to alter the trump suit, in which case no point is awarded. If the latter, he must deal each player three more cards and then turn ▪

up the next card to determine the new trump suit. (Once again, should a Knave show, the Dealer receives one *GRATIS* point.) Should the new trump card be of the same suit as its predecessor, the Dealer gives each player a further three cards, and turns up the next; and so on, until a new suit has been agreed upon.

Play starts with each player disposing of unwanted cards until he has six remaining in his hand; the procedure is then the same as for Whist. At the end of the hand, the tricks are turned up and scores awarded. One point, for *"game,"* is awarded to the player who has taken the highest total value of cards in his tricks: this total is calculated by evaluating the Tens as ten notches, the Aces as four, the Kings as three, the Queens as two, and the Knaves as one. Other points, one apiece, are awarded for *"high"* (to the player who was dealt the highest trump), a *"low"* (to him dealt the lowest trump) and a *"Jack"* (for the possession of the Knave of the trump suit in a trick). The first player to score seven points

triumphs. Should two players attain seven points together, the points are recounted in the order: *HIGH, LOW, JACK* and *GAME*, and the first to reach seven in this counting being declared winner.

For four players, the play is in partnerships, the partners facing each other. The establishment of the trump suit is conducted only between the Dealer and the player to his left; the other two players are forbidden to look at their cards until the trump suit has been determined. Aside from this, play is as for two or three.

CALIFORNIA LOO

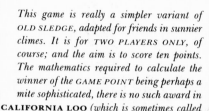

This game is really a simpler variant of
OLD SLEDGE, adapted for friends in sunnier
climes. It is for TWO PLAYERS ONLY, of
course; and the aim is to score ten points.
The mathematics required to calculate the
winner of the GAME POINT being perhaps a
mite sophisticated, there is no such award in
CALIFORNIA LOO (which is sometimes called
CALIFORNIA JACK), but HIGH, LOW and
JACK are granted for, respectively, the
highest and lowest trumps found among
the tricks, and for the Knave of trumps.

Play as for Old Sledge, but with the procedure differing slightly: There is no nego-
tiation for the establishment of the trump
suit; presumably lest suave debate should
lead to an exchange of blows. The Dealer
gains no extra point should the card in question
be a Knave or Jack. At the end of each
trick, each player takes a fresh card from
stock, and then another is
turned up, to establish a
new trump suit for the
ensuing trick.

KLABBERJASS

THIS GAME FOR TWO PLAYERS is believed to have come to us from **THE DUTCH**, but is nevertheless a pleasant enough diversion; perhaps it was taken to the Low Lands centuries ago from our own shores, and has now returned to its rightful home. We shall probably never know the TRUTH OF THE MATTER, alas.

The object is to be the first to score either three hundred or five hundred points, depending upon prior agreement. As with *Piquet*, the Deuces, Treys, Fours, Fives and Sixes are discarded from the pack, so that thirty-two cards remain. After shuffling, the players cut; the dealership is awarded to him with the lower card; but the dealership alternates between the two for succeeding hands. The Dealer gives six cards to each, three by three (these are all the cards for play); and then the next card is turned face upwards, its suit denoting the *trump suit*. The player who has not dealt (whom we shall call the ELDER HAND, after *Piquet's* example) may then say: "ACCEPT," to signify that he accepts that trump suit; or "PASS," thereby permitting the Dealer to ask for a different trump; or ☛

"SCHMEISS" *(pronounced to rhyme with "mice")*, which is an offer to the Dealer to reject the hand, reshuffle, and start again. If the ELDER HAND has said: "Pass," the Dealer may simply say: "Accept," but alternatively he too may say "Schmeiss," with significance as before.

The trump suit established, the players attempt to score with their best sequences, as in Piquet; but the reader should note that the ranking of cards in **KLABBERJASS** is different from that in its more august fellow – indeed, different from that in any other card game known to me. In the trump suit alone, the ranking is, in descending order: Knave or "Jack,"

Nine, Ace, Ten, King, Queen, Eight, Seven. In the other suits the order is: Ace, Ten, King, Queen, Knave, Nine, Eight, Seven. Not without cause is the Dutch mentality adjudged inscrutable! To return to our calling of the sequences. This is initiated by the Elder Hand, who tells the Dealer of his highest-scoring sequence (or "MELD"): twenty points are allotted for a meld of three cards; fifty for one of four or more cards. On hearing the ELDER HAND'S claim, the Dealer may say: "Good" (he cannot contest the issue), "No Good" (he has a higher-value meld, which he must show and for which he scores), or "Same" (he has an equal-value meld, in which case the issue is determined by the higher top card of the two melds; or, if one is in the

trump suit, it automatically prevails; or,
if both are equal in all respects, the
Elder Hand's is deemed the better, and
receives the requisite points accord-
ingly). Only one player may score in
this way; but, once his meld has
emerged victorious from the bidding,
he may then score for all other melds
in his hand.

Play now commences. The Elder
Hand leads the first card. Play is
much as in Piquet, but with an
important distinction. If a player has no cards in the suit that
has been led but does possess cards in the trump suit, he is
OBLIGED TO use them. Any player who has both the King and
Queen of the trump suit is said to have a "BELLA;" and is
granted twenty points on playing the second of these cards.

Once the cards have been played out, the players turn their
attentions to their tricks. The number of tricks each has taken
is immaterial when awarding points. Instead the search is on
for special cards gained, and these are evaluated as follows:
JASS (Knave of the trump suit) twenty points; MENEL (Nine of
the trump suit) fourteen; Aces eleven; Tens ten; Kings four;
Queens three; non-trump Knaves two.

BLACK LADY
HEARTS

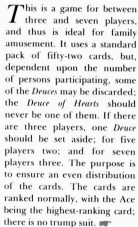

This is a game for between three and seven players, and thus is ideal for family amusement. It uses a standard pack of fifty-two cards, but, dependent upon the number of persons participating, some of the *Deuces* may be discarded; the *Deuce of Hearts* should never be one of them. If there are three players, one *Deuce* should be set aside; for five players two; and for seven players three. The purpose is to ensure an even distribution of the cards. The cards are ranked normally, with the Ace being the highest-ranking card; there is no trump suit. 🍃

The method of play is like WHIST. Players must if feasible follow the suit of the led card; failure to do so is termed *"REVOKING,"* and is punished by a penalty of thirteen points and the declaration of the hand to be void. If the hand is normal, at its end players must examine their tricks; and incur a penalty of one point for each *HEARTS* card therein; moreover, possession of the *QUEEN OF SPADES* invokes a penalty of thirteen points. There is no other scoring. The winner is he who, after an agreed number of hands, or when the players decide to quit the game, has the lowest score.

In a simpler version of the

game, the Queen of Spades is treated as would be any other card. In yet a different form, scores are counted according to the values of the Hearts card, such that the King incurs thirteen penalty points; a Queen twelve; and so on. In some regional versions it is also possible for a player to reduce his penalty score by possessing certain cards in the tricks won – such as the *NINE OF DIAMONDS*.

CANASTA

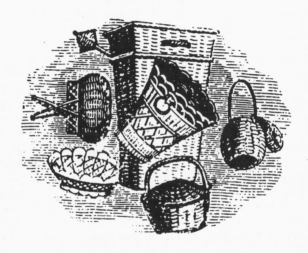

This is a game for four people, playing in two partnerships of two, the partners facing each other; and details of it have been sent to me by a correspondent as far afield as Uruguay; so far as I am aware, it is not practised in our own country; which seems a shame for it is more than moderately enjoyable to play. Perhaps its inclusion here will enhance

its popularity. Its name is the Spanish word for *"basket,"* because so many cards – a whole basketful! – are required for the playing of the game. We use a hundred and eight cards, when all is told: two complete packs of fifty-two cards, as well as their four JOKERS; all shuffled together. In this game, all Jokers and Deuces are **"WILD CARDS,"** which is to say that they can assume any value required by their holder; as we shall see.

After cutting to establish the dealership, each player is dealt eleven cards, one by one, in the usual way. The remaining cards comprise the STOCK; and they are placed in a neat heap, face downwards, in the centre of the playing area. The top card is turned up and placed beside this heap, to act as the first card of the DISCARD PILE.

Any player who discovers that he has been dealt a red Trey must forthwith lay it face upwards on the table in front of him; and replenish his hand from the stock: for, as we shall see, these red Treys are worth a great number of points. ❦

This done, play proper is set to commence. The player to the dealer's left initiates the play by taking the top card from the stock. Using the cards that are now in his hand, he must try to make as many MELDS as he is able; and set them down, face upwards, on the table in front of him. A meld is a set of three or more cards all having the same value (for instance, four Knaves or Jacks, or three Fours); a *CANASTA* is a meld of seven cards. Each meld must contain no more than three Wild Cards making up its number; and must also possess at least two "*natural*" cards of the required value.

Treys cannot normally be melded; indeed, as at the start, red Treys cannot at all, but must be laid out immediately on receipt and replaced in the player's hand from the stock (unless gained from the discard pile, in which case they are not replaced): black Treys can only be melded at the end, when a player is going out; and then not with Wild Cards. The first meld that a partnership sets down must be of value at least fifty points (see below for scoring).

A player may choose (but not if his partnership has yet to make a meld) not to take the top card of the stock if he sees that he can use the exposed card of the discard pile to complete a meld using other cards in his hand. If he does this, he must take all of the cards in

that pile; after he has used as many as possible to create new melds or to add to his existing ones, the remaining cards become part of his hand. Thus a player should consider carefully the advantages and disadvantages of this course of action before taking it. Should the exposed card of the discard heap be a black Trey, then that heap is *"frozen;"* and may not be utilised by any player ☞

until the black Trey is covered. The pile is also frozen if it contains a Wild Card or a red Trey, further discards being placed crossways above it; and it remains *"frozen"* until a player can withdraw either the Wild Card or the exposed card and meld it with two natural cards he possesses in his hand.

Once a player has finished making or supplementing his own melds, and perhaps also supplementing the melds that his partner has laid out, he finishes his turn by jettisoning a single card on to the discard pile. Play is then taken up by the player to his left.

The aim of the enterprise is for the partnership to be first to accumulate five thousand points in the form of melds and Treys. Players may choose to go out (which is to say, to leave themselves with no cards in their hand), but only if their partnership has attained at least one *CANASTA*. Scoring is as follows:

Each Joker	50 POINTS
Each Deuce or Ace	20 POINTS
Each Eight, Nine, Ten, Knave (Jack),	
Queen or King	10 POINTS
Each Four, Five, Six, or Seven	5 POINTS
Each black Trey	5 POINTS
Each red Trey	100 POINTS

But all four red Treys	800 POINTS
Each natural *canasta* (that is, with no	
Wild Cards)	500 POINTS
Each mixed *canasta*	300 POINTS
Going out	100 POINTS

FAN TAN

I have more than once in these pages made clear my personal views on the use of card games for gambling; yet **FAN TAN** *is indeed a gambling game, as its alternative name,* "PLAY OR PAY", *makes brazen. My purpose is to indicate, briefly, that even such games can be adapted to give harmless pleasure to the innocent. Here, then, is an appropriately sanitized version.*

As many players as wish may partake; a standard pack of fifty-two cards is used; and the aim is to be the first player to use up all his cards. After a Dealer has been selected, he deals the cards CLOCKWISE *around the circle; some players will have one card more than others; but, as the dealership passes clockwise at the end of each hand, this disadvantage evens out over several hands.*

The player to the Dealer's left lays a seven in the centre of the area; if he is unable so to do, play passes to the next player clockwise; until a Seven is laid. The next player may lay another Seven to either

side of this one; or, matching the suit, an Eight above the original Seven, or a Six below it; each player laying no more than one card at a time. As the game progresses around and around the circle, all four Sevens come out, and columns are built upwards from each of them, in suits, to their Kings, and downwards to their Aces.

The game, in this form, can be played by **young and old alike**, with considerable delight, and without any possibility of an affront to the proper sensibilities. Only an instrument of OLD NICK would seek to wager on his becoming the first to divest himself of all his cards.

GLOSSARY:
BEING the LANGUAGE *of* CARD-PLAYERS

*E*ven in genteel society, card-players use some words that may not be familiar to those who, prior to having perused within this book, had conceived that card games were, in Mr. Alex. Steward's oft-quoted words from his *VILLAINS' BIBLE*,

... the very *tentacles* of Damnation itself; reaching up from the *Blackest* Pits of vile foulness; *liches* of lost souls; the *mucor* of the mind; bestiality beyond all known *bounds* of comprehension ...

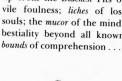

Ace: A One.

Cut: To divide the pack into two parts and place the bottom part of the pack on top. This is done, usually by the player to the Dealer's right, after the pack has been shuffled.

Deal: To distribute the cards in the manner required to begin the game. Cards are usually dealt one at a time, face downwards, from the top of the deck; beginning with the player to the Dealer's left and thence going clockwise.

Deck: An obnoxious neologism meaning pack (q.v.).

Deuce: A Two.

Elder Hand: The first player to receive cards from the Dealer.

Foundation: In patience games, or solitaires, the first card laid ready to receive the sequential cards in the different suits.

Hand: (1) The full number of cards required by each player for the game to begin. (2) A single round of game.

Jack: SEE Knave.

Jokers: Extra cards, usually set
  aside before play, but in
  some games required as wild
  cards (q.v.).

Knave: The lowest ranking
  Court card; the prince. Also
  known as Jack.

Meld: A scoring combination
  of cards. Usually, in those
  games involving melds, a
  sequence of three or more
  cards of the same suit in
  continuous ranked order; or
  three or four cards of the
  same value.

Pack: A standard pack of cards
  has fifty-two cards, arranged
  in four suits of thirteen cards
  each; in addition, usually two
  jokers (q.v.).

Packet: Term used to describe
  a pile of cards.

Reserve: A pile of cards set
  aside for later use.

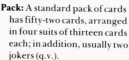

Shuffle: To arrange the cards in a random order. Any player may shuffle the cards before cutting or dealing, but the Dealer can elect to be the last to do so.

Stock: The cards remaining after a hand has been dealt to all players.

Suits: The four sets of cards in the pack; they are: Spades; Hearts; Diamonds; Clubs.

Trey: A Three.

Trick: The cards from one round of the game, one card having been contributed by each player.

Trump: A card or suit designated, in some games, always to have higher rank than others.

Wild Cards: Cards that can be given any rank or suit specified by their holder.

FINIS